ACROSS THE HIGH DIVIDE

For Sally —

never stop wanting more

Good wishes!

Laurie

Across the High Divide

New Poems

LAURIE WAGNER BUYER

GRp

Ghost Road Press
Denver, Colorado

Many thanks to the following publishers and publications in which these poems first appeared, sometimes in earlier versions:

"Sleeping with the River," *Side Canyons*, Five Star Publishing
"His Horses," *Cowboy Poetry: The Reunion,* Gibbs Smith
"Sunderance," *Cowboy Poetry Matters: From Abilene to the Mainstream,* Story Line Press
"Range Storm," Mountain Gazette
"Outline," and "Refuge," The Fence Post

Library of Congress Cataloging-in-Publication Data.
Wagner Buyer, Laurie (1954 —).
Across the High Divide.
Ghost Road Press
ISBN 0-9771272-5-7 (Trade Paperback)
Library of Congress Control Number: 2005937309

Book Design: Sonya Unrein

Ghost Road Press
Denver, Colorado
ghostroadpress.com

ACKNOWLEDGMENTS

With gratitude to beloved friends: Alfred for wise guidance; Joanne for the long walks and talks; Chris and Pat for teaching me about amazon women; Page for encouraging me on this difficult path; Matt for being a faithful brother; Kathlene for years of generous mentoring; and Carlos, *mi amor*, for taking me to the summit and beyond.

And to Sonya and Matt for their enthusiastic, dedicated vision of poetry in our art-starved world.

For the ones who tried, but didn't make it

Bob, Sy, Laurie Jo, Jeb

CONTENTS

RUNNING OUT OF THREAD

SLEEPING WITH THE RIVER

RUNNING OUT OF THREAD

"Chains do not hold a marriage together.
It is threads, hundreds of tiny threads,
which sew people together through the years."

—Simone Signoret

SELLING GUNS

"...determined to do
the only thing you could do—
determined to save
the only life you could save."
      —Mary Oliver, "The Journey"

At the age of forty-eight
on the edge of insanity
on the verge of divorce after twenty years
I pull into a parking lot behind Kodiak Firearms
going against the yellow arrow
and realize too late that a Jeep Liberty can't be parked
at this impossible ass-backwards angle.
I put my head on the steering wheel and sigh.
My attempt to back out is blocked by a Ford Powerstroke,
a dark-blue diesel with two t-shirted teenagers
who think I'm an air-head.

What they don't know won't hurt them.

At age twenty I learned to shoot
because it was required in the wilderness
where rifles, hanging in six-point antler racks,
decorated the door and window frames of the log homestead
where I'd come to live with a bearded, buckskinned
believer in independence and individual freedom.

I wave an apathetic apology
complete an agonizing three-point turn
between parked Toyotas and Subarus
and exit through the entrance
circle the block and try again
this time dutifully following directions.
I park with perfection, pocket the keys
and pick up the rifle in its fake-leather case
and the Ruger still in its original box.

It's a sunny day, bright for December,
enough chill for a vest, but not a jacket.
I walk across the paved lot to the store's back door
where a sign states: please use front entrance.
I feel funny packing firearms on a city street.
I'm uneasy, sense something criminal
in the way I stroll with nonchalance up the concrete walk,
as if an aging woman in black slacks, black turtleneck,
turquoise vest with black trim, black socks, and moccasins,
hair upswept in a tangled twist, with silver earrings and guns
is a common occurrence here.

The harsh blast of a buzzer sounds my entrance.

The small store is crowded:
the two teenagers pace the place,
a man waits with a rifle case,
a stocky guy and his bleach-blonde gal peruse pistols
as if they were an assortment of wedding rings.
The owner behind the counter,
presumably the person I spoke with on the phone,
argues with an overweight, ball-capped aficionado
wearing Converse tennis shoes and faded, fat-stressed jeans:

"The price is the price. I can't knock anything off.
I've only got twenty in over what I paid for it."
"Well," the buyer says, tugging his Case cap,
"then let me see the Blackhawk in the box."
The owner nods at me, and says, "be with you in a moment,"
but seeing anxiety in my eyes he reaches for the rifle case
and says, "Laurie? You called?"
I smile "yes" and he says,
"Give me just a minute to check these out."
I hand over the pistol with its brand-new
hand-stitched holster and extra shell holder.

I wipe sweaty palms on my thighs and walk the glass display cases,
studying models and prices,
examining assault rifles and old Colts like I care,
like I'm truly interested. I'm not. I want out.
I want to be anywhere except in this too-hot store surrounded by guns.
I want to be away from my suffocating edge of anger.

With his volatile nature and hair-trigger temper,
my father always apologized afterwards, always said,
"That's why I won't have a gun in the house,"
and yet, for Christmas, 1975,
he bought me the sleek Browning .22 with scope
after I'd spent my first year homesteading across the river from Canada.
He'd ordered it and had it held at the hardware store
because, snowbound, it was five long months
before I got shoveled out and into town.

The owner banters with Ball-cap.
He asks the couple in love if they need help
and they say, smiling, "no, just looking,"
then amble out hand in hand.
I want to tell them that a pistol won't protect them,
won't keep the wolf from the door,
won't prevent Peter from pursuing Paula even if she is married.
I want to say, "buy her twenty years worth of flowers instead,
buy him football tickets."

I take a seat on the only chair and close my weary eyes.
I don't want to look at ranks of rifles or mounted elk heads.
I listen to Ball-cap pontificate:
"The Uzi I bought off that biker was a piece of shit...
Are you sure you can't knock off something?
What about throwing in a couple boxes of shells?"

I sense a presence too close and my eyes tear open.
The man with the rifle has set it on the counter
and he's trying to look at the 9 mm with extra clip.
I cross my legs the other way and murmur "sorry."
I don't close my eyes again. I stare at the toes of my shoes
and wonder why the left moccasin isn't tied the same way as the right.
I calculate the amount of money I'll receive,
think of the gifts I'll buy for my mother, my sisters, my girl friends.

The owner slips my .22 from its case,
levers it to make sure it's unloaded,
then looks down the barrel.
"You've got critters living in here," he says,
"a whole colony complete with cobwebs."
"I know," I say, "it hasn't been cleaned in years."

What he doesn't know won't hurt him—that the Browning
hasn't been cleaned since Sy shot himself in '93,
a too-close-for-comfort reminder of Bob's suicide in '77.

"It never had much use," I explain, "just for gophers
and goats I butchered. Some target practice."

I was never any good—"Christ, you can't hit
the broadside of the barn even with a scope.
It's sad you've got such crappy eyes"—
But, I didn't care.
He couldn't make me cry anymore and
I knew I could kill something if I had to—
after all, he was a good teacher in many ways
and the day we pulled out of the place,
the spring after we found Bob's note and the .25-.20 gone,
I was the one who shot the dog and the cats
because there was no one to take care of them,
no way to take them along.
If you ask me the hardest part was washing
the bloody clothes picked up from the funeral parlor.

It only takes one shot to kill a man,
but even after all these years it's bothered me
how he did it lying on his back in the crawl space of a cabin,
the floor joists and spiders right in his face.
I buried the dog, but I just threw the cats in the brush,
dusted off my hands and walked away, never even looked back.

"No," I say, "It's never been fired. Bought it new in '83."

The store owner spins the chamber on the .38-.357.
Sunlight glints off the snub-nosed silver barrel
that was specially shortened to fit a woman's hand.
"I bought it for a reason, but never needed it."

Foolish thing to say.
He'll think I meant to kill someone.
Someone who didn't treat me nice and he'd be right.
I used to dream the same nightmare over and over again—
sitting on a witness stand saying to the scowling judge:
"I had no choice. He was in such misery."

And when I was angry, my father's child,
when I hurt so bad that the blood boiled,
pounding against my brain,
I used to excuse myself by accusing him:
"It's your fault you stupid son-of-a-bitch,
you're the one who taught me how to do it..."
But some saving grace would surface
and I'd hear my mother saying "Frank, Frank"
then my fury would die and then I'd cry.

Ball-cap is staring at me.
I narrow my eyes and he turns away to fondle the Blackhawk,
digging the toe of his tennis shoe into the carpet.
The owner shrugs as if to say it doesn't matter
and begins flipping pages in a thick reference book.

The teenagers are gone.
The man with the rifle waits, tapping his fingers
in time to the country music wafting from the back.
"Give me just a couple more minutes," the owner says to him.
"No problem," he replies, "I'm not in any hurry."

I am. I'm in a huge hurry. I want my money.
I want something to show for fifty years of trying to stay alive,
trying to find my way through the not so clean streets of my soul.
I want to get out into the air where I can breathe again,
where I won't hear him saying, "He's down. He's done.
Get me the .30-.30"...or see him standing in the snow,
the open-sight rifle propped against an aspen
as he levered in a shell and shot the colt
I'd petted and pampered since the day he was born.

Minutes click by, soaking me in sweat, leave me trembling.
I haven't eaten. Why didn't I eat?
It started out as a good day.
I woke up happy, went to work in my writing room,
went for a long walk, went for the mail.
When did everything begin to go downhill?
When I got the guns out from behind my mother's couch
where I'd stashed them the night I came to live with her?
When I walked in this store and the buzzer sounded
some start to reliving every awful event of my life?

It wasn't just the colt, or mild-tempered Ahkee,
Jack the blind draft horse gelding,
the heifer who tested positive for Bangs,
marauding coyotes and wounded elk,
the countless cows crippled in one way or another,
old faithful Sam, howling and barking in pain,
or Sy, who sought some sort of relief through the rifle's black eye,
or Jeb and Laurie Jo and the jealous bullet that brought them down,
no it was the spiral of depression that shadowed us,
the fear that you'd be next on the list.

What does a woman do when she asks "what's wrong"
and the answer is "nothing?"
What does she do when she attempts an embrace and is pushed away?
What does she do when something can't be fixed,
can't be mended, can't be changed?
What does she do when her husband tells her, "I never trusted you
and I don't believe you ever loved me?"

I want to know how she's supposed to go on.

"Here's what we've got," the owner says,
coming around the counter to meet me half-way.
On a pad of paper he's written some numbers:
"The rifle's got a little rust and needs work
so I figured it at eighty percent of book...
the pistol's good, figured that at ninety-eight.
Here's what they're worth to me."

The amount is only half of what I imagined it might be.
Panic chokes off my air. It's not enough.
It will never be enough, but I settle for what's offered
because I don't have the energy to do anything else.
How else do I go on, find a way to stay alive?

"I'll take it," I say.
The owner seems surprised when I don't barter.
He looks embarrassed.
He starts to say something, but I cut him off.
"I just don't want them anymore. I want to get rid of them."
"Okay," he says, "let me see your driver's license and I'll get you a check."

I stand there and fumble with foam ear plugs: two pair for a dollar.
I pick out four plastic packs and take two singles out of my wallet.
Ball-cap is waiting.
The man with the rifle is waiting.

The buzzer sounds and I watch a young woman in tight Levi's
and a spangled red and black oversize sweater survey accessories.
I bet she's looking for a Christmas gift for her boyfriend.
I study the ear plugs I'm buying for you for your birthday.
A silly gift, but something I know you'll use
while four-wheeling to check the horses
or plowing the road to the house where you now live alone.

Why couldn't I get the guns out of my head?
Was it all the times I heard you say with frustration,
"If it gets any worse I guess I'll just get the gun."
Kidney disease, slow but certain killer, wasn't a welcome fate.
I used to go out for my walks and wonder
if you'd still be sitting silent in your chair,
or if I'd find a note, you and a rifle gone.
And when it got worse, I shied from the thought
that in a helpless rage you'd take us both out.

When did the voice in my head quit saying stay and work it out,
you have enough love, enough acceptance, enough forgiveness.
When did that voice begin to shout
get out, get out, get out, before it's too late!

The owner hands me a check.
I push over the earplugs and say, "I'll take these."
"Two dollars," he says.
"Tax?" I ask.
"No tax. We'll just forget the tax."

I see it in his eyes. He knows he's cheated me.
He hasn't given me what the guns are worth,
but he can't backtrack now. None of us can.
But it doesn't matter.
While the guns are gone, memory remains.
I stuff the check in my pocket, say "thanks,"
and rush out, gulping raw life-affirming air
as I try to get back to the Jeep without collapsing.

I tell myself it wasn't that bad,
that I imagined I found you sitting fully clothed
in your dark recliner in the middle of the night,
the bedroom light burning bright on the bed
where you'd tossed and turned and could not sleep,
the unlocked gun cabinet twenty feet away.
Perhaps you had a right to hate me, to want me out of your life,
but when I tried to talk, tried to help,
tried to find a way for us to go on,
you told me through clenched teeth that I was killing you,
that I was the reason you were dying.

Was it that awful?
Did I feel the strangled tightness in my throat
that kept me cowering under the covers
in a single bed in the spare room
when your wrath was everywhere,
palpable as wading through muck,
the fetid closeness of death flaring my nostrils
as I lay without moving, waiting for morning,
listening for the sound of carpet-hushed footsteps
the swish-click of the .30-.06 being levered?

When I crawl into the driver's seat,
the Liberty's warm from winter sun
beaming through the windshield.
I slip the key into the ignition,
but before I can start the engine
tears ignite in my tired eyes.
Hands clenched close to wet cheeks,
I press my head to the wheel,
and turn loose the long held lament.

My father's gone.
Bob's gone.
Sy's gone.
Laurie Jo and Jeb are gone.
The ranch I loved is gone from me
and I am gone from you.
Now, my guns are gone,
but we are both still alive.

VICTIM OF CIRCUMSTANCE

Young, so young, too young to know the truth about mistrust
and how it eats away the core of love like an overripe apple.

I never knew he came to you with poisoned words,
his last attempt to tear us apart before we ever started:

"You're too old. She's young and pretty, talented and smart.
She'll never stay. She'll leave you, by God, the way that she left me."

For twenty years I asked, "What's wrong?" and you said, "nothing."
For twenty years I poured myself into that festering hole in your heart.

If only you would had told me. I could have cut out the bad part,
could have salvaged the sweet fruit of what we'd been to each other.

But you shut me out, kept me in the dark, turned away, wouldn't talk,
until his prophecy, spoiling in self-fulfilling truth, split us in two.

SNAPPED FROM THE STEM

The dying deceived me—
that brown brittleness that begins
along the edges of a leaf
just before it curls inward on itself.

I did not know we were so far gone
until I struggled to kiss your dry lips
and felt you snap from the stem
of our weather-worn branch of loving.

RANGE STORM

Cell-like, frail clouds bump and clot
forming a white mass above the mountains
until the high peaks of the Divide disappear
as if the rocks and cliffs were never there.

It snows steady, filling crevasses and ravines
above timberline where the air thins to near
nothingness, where the sun forgets for days
it's scheduled to appear, rise and shine.

Watching from the foggy ranch house window,
I see myself stranded by the sudden storm,
lost in the whining wind with no direction,
no idea how to find my way home to you.

CRADLE OF ARMS

Every day the wind beats me
bruising my tender brain until
parts turn black and blue,
edges purpling toward
an unsightly olive green
and even the briefest lull
leaves the ominous echo
of bass drums pounding.

Every night the wind rocks
the drafty river bottom house,
but this is no lullaby,
no soothing ease to slip
into sleep and dreams.

I crave a cradle of arms, an unbreakable bough.

Not so very big, not all that grown up,
I am still child enough to cry, "hold me,
lift me into your lap, sing away the wind."

BOAR BRISTLE BRUSH

Life laughed at the capricious styling of my hair,
slicked back in a whorled bun,
or loosened in a storm that stirred
the strands in crazy disarray.

I searched for the right brush
to balance my temperamental load,
one to curry wildness while leaving
the corona of the mane untamed.

Holding a rosewood handle,
my fingers curled around the polished shaft,
I found the perfect instrument
for curls, braids, ringlets and waves.

Bristle stiff, the brush seduced
the scalp with sharp tenderness,
lifted snarls from a sensitive psyche
as static electricity sparked latent desire.

Unbinding my blonde hair,
I shook it across my shoulders
and handed you the brush
which you studied, then set aside
inducing my new self image
to sigh once, then die.

EDGING TOWARD THE END

I taste the dying on your lips, the tender burn, the little sips
of life left hanging in the folds of what we never say.
I hold fast to what remains unsaid,
the false romance put to bed along with other lies we've told,
the fantasies we bought and sold like trinkets at the local fair.

No argument, husband, spare me the hasty grave
of blank despair, the black on black I dare not wear.
I'll leave my grievances where they always lay,
in silences discarded by the road, gestures never made,
lost seductions tangled with songs left unsung.

Instead, give me your swollen tongue still searching for a way
to speak, your eyes grown distant, weak with longing,
wanting yet to stay. Give me what you can. Give me today.

CREEKSIDE

Among fragrant bedstraw, shooting stars blaze
between wild onions, iris, geranium, blue flax—

colors stirring the consciousness of another drought year.
How can they bloom with rain so scarce the stream barely runs?

Narcissus anemones nod next to elegant camas and mariposa tulips.
Paintbrush and Rocky Mountain lilies vie for a shocking shade of orange.

Queen Anne's lace, yellow banner, spotted saxifrage, miner's candle,
fairy trumpets and fireweed—each a brief celebration.

Along the shadowed bank, heartleaf bittercress alludes to the truth
that scent and shape don't always match the reality of taste and touch.

How can we survive when words are so rare we startle the dog when we speak
Yet, our love lingers, fragrant as the flowers we crush beneath our feet.

RUNNING OUT OF THREAD

Like thighs pressed tight
to the inside seams of jeans
we rubbed against each other
wearing one another thin
until we were both thread bare.

When the silk spool of love ran out,
I turned to the everyday cotton
of just taking care of things,
to the heavy carpet cord of compassion,
to the rough jute of desperation
which wouldn't fit through
the tiny eye of our anger.

Too close to the confusion,
I couldn't see to thread the needle,
couldn't find enough scraps
of faded flannel comfort,
or tough denim determination
to mend the countless holes.

When even twine couldn't bind us,
I quit trying to patch the widening tear,
stopped wanting to cover our exposed skin.

I ceased sewing
and let us
unravel.

ONE MORE ATTEMPT

I'm sipping bourbon and seven,
something I've never done before,
but my throat's sore from not speaking,
from not saying what I've needed to say for years.
Can you hear me through the tenor of the television,
the bass roar of the bull riders,
the soprano of the raving statesman,
the alto of the ill-equipped weather woman
who doesn't know if tomorrow will bring rain?
The strain's diminished me to a nothingness I can't bear.
I don't care if what I say will upset you or make you hate me.
I couldn't cry if I wanted to because all my tears went to town.

Why don't you know that I need you to love me,
to be the most important, most worthy thing in your life,
more than a wife, a balanced center from which everything turns.
Feeble. Lame. But isn't it the same as believing I could be something
more than a door you walk through on your way to work.
No, you're not a jerk at all, but I'm telling you that if you don't talk to me
that I'm going to fall apart. Whose heart? Mine,
unless behind that blinking confused stare you think I still care.
But I did once, didn't I? Tried to make your dreams come true,
paid the price of being sacrosanct, something so rare
you wouldn't dare make me a common reoccurrence of lust.

Okay. Nothing to say? That's fine.
I'll take my troubles on down the road to Wichita where life's fair.
I hear they're looking for waitresses there.

RIDING BITTERNESS

Bent over her outstretched neck
the stink of old sweat strong
I ride my bitterness—hard—
eyes inches from pinned ears
vision whipped by knotted mane
bit foam flecking my face
spurs raking blood-streaked flanks
quirt raised, ready to lash
the heaving hindquarters
that drive me faster and faster
into the sweet nightmare
of never going home again.

DETOX

Sure, say it:
been there, done that—
all over now
so move on...

To what?

Kneeling on shards
kissing icy porcelain
hours of retching
the cramps and pain
nothing compared to
the shiver misery
that lasts all night.

Dawn light sanctifies
twenty lost years
my wet and bloody body
curled naked on the cold floor
like an infant with no swaddling clothes.

WHERE IS THE PLACE

"If you should die, where is the place
that I will call home?"
    — William Reichard, "A Widow's Song"

Death dawdles at the door
comes to knock
turns away
returns to ring the bell
decides to stay awhile.

I don't serve tea and cookies.
I sit and stare
wonder where he got that smug look
ponder how he found our house
so far from anywhere.

I leave.
He follows me into the yard
down the driveway
along the highway.
He follows me far away from you.

You live alone now
and death quit calling.
He's too busy tagging my heels
looking for an easy answer
which I refuse to give

because there is no answer
only the question
which I ask over and over again
in the difficult dark
awake in the night
sleeping without you.

SAYING GOOD-BYE FOR THE
HUNDREDTH TIME

This time the dog doesn't try to leap in my Jeep
when he realizes I won't be staying.

He sits by my feet, presses his head against my knee
as I scratch his dappled ear and whisper "it's okay."

This time we don't cling or cry, we barely hug
as sorrow sweeps past us on a sudden gust of wind.

You turn to split stove kindling in the setting sun.
I slip behind the wheel and roll slow up the driveway.

For the longest time I sit on the road trying not to count
our uncountable losses, the good-byes that make us grieve.

Then, a bluebird, a flitting scrap of cerulean, crosses
my field of vision, lights on a leaning fence post,

and gives me reason to pull through the steel gate,
trusting that the dust I leave behind will settle in time.

"I KNEW IF I GAVE YOU ENOUGH ROPE YOU'D HANG YOURSELF"

Ropes woke me this morning—
thin rope, thick rope, slick rope, rough rope
jute, nylon, cotton, hemp, rawhide
clothesline, lariat, tow rope, macramé cord

ropes that hoist sails aloft
ropes that belay climbers
ropes that tie packs on saddles
ropes that pull people to safety

ropes that break a colt's spirit
ropes that choke down cows
ropes that drag calves to the fire
ropes that tie hands and feet

ropes that sing, vibrating in a gale
ropes that hold tender shoots to trellis
ropes that pull the small red wagon
ropes the smitten kitten chases

ropes that twist and knot and snag
ropes that take the heavy weight
ropes that never rot never break
ropes that wish they'd never been made

Bless be the tie that binds my heart...

I'll take the rope you gave me
throw it over a tall branch
loop it under a piece of board
and make myself a child's swing.

STAKE RACE

A thoroughbred-cross filly
on an old draft horse outfit,
I never held up well,
couldn't pull the weight or carry a load.

Thin-skinned, fragile-hooved,
I couldn't take below-zero cold
or steep rock-studded slopes.
I wanted thick blankets and warm mash,
not frozen bunch grass and river water turned to ice.

I never did figure out how to turn tail to the wind.

Flighty, unpredictable,
I slunk my colts and cribbed on words,
fought the bit, sulked under the whip,
and paced nervous tracings
around the high pole pen.

Never sweet tempered,
I kicked when cornered,
reared if tied too tight,
ran away every chance I got,
even nipped the hand that fed me.

I tried to be an easy keeper
but I ate out of boredom,
losing my fancy palomino gloss
to high-altitude desert sun.

Sure I had flaws—
not long-legged enough,
narrow in the chest, a bit swaybacked,
but I was never a shy breeder or a bitchy bell mare.

All I needed was a chance
to do what I was born to do:
run full out, breathless, heart bursting,
tearing up every day's oval track
with an undeniable desire to win,
show my stuff, hear the cheers,
push myself in a passionate effort
to flash first across the finish line
wearing the Valentine red silks
of someone who would love me
for being a once in a lifetime long shot.

HIS HORSES

I do not dream of him or the way he once held me.
I dream of him and his horses—

their names sliding through fingers of consciousness
like butter-soft reins on a worn-out summer day—

Peanuts, Diamond, Blackie, Buck, Duchess, Claude,
Tequila, Bill, Honda, Shavano, Honeybee, Ned...

He swings a saddle, settles it on a humped-up back,
vapor puffs from flared nostrils as he reaches for the cinch.

He sticks a spurred boot into a stirrup and is gone,
riding into another sunrise to chase down a herd of chores.

Slats, Socks, Smoke, Booger Red, Blue, Billy Bars,
Rastus, Poco, Wink, Jake, Keno, Dancer...

He heaves on a harness, the hames high over his head,
a velvet nose buried in the grain box as he adjusts the britchin'.

Not easy to hold them in and keep their heads up, his hands
slip on thick four-up lines stiff with twenty-below cold—

Pat and Mike, Stubby and Dick, Nell and Bell, Tom and Molly,
Donnie and Clyde, Jack and Jill, Hoss and Boss...

He counts wrecks the way some people count birthdays,
each one a reminder that it's a miracle he's still alive.

I do not think of him and the way he once loved me.
I think of him and his horses—

their names echoing over the winter meadows as he stands
pitchfork in hand near the pole corral calling at dawn:

Amigo, Dunny, Brandy...Cookie...Candy.

SLEEPING WITH THE RIVER

"We cannot discover ourselves without
first discovering the universe, the earth,
and the imperatives of our own being."
—Thomas Berry

BREAKING TRAIL

In winter woods
a snowshoe hare hides
beside an aspen trunk
white fur and brown
blend into snow
and blue-shadowed light filters
through twigs and limbs
in dappled disarray.

A chickadee twitters
from tree to tree
no other sound except
the breathing breath of evening wind
that wanders in whorls about my face
and talks of other trails I've made

through snowfalls such as this
softened by sun into sugar-spun drifts,
wind packed into waves
as hard as sea salt,
crusty as weathered brine.

This unmarred earth is mine for now,
but in the dark part of twilight
others will follow my new trail,
the evening elk and demure deer,
coyotes and cottontails,
even field mice, their precise tracks
stitching rabbit brush to sage brush
as they seek out autumn's sown seeds.

NIMBUS

Two mornings short of solstice
uniform gray drapes the day
and the entire sky,
gravid with watery air,
presses against my chest
as I trudge uphill into a squall
sliding off the high divide.

Stinging snow strikes full in the face
forcing me to whirl and kneel,
while tears, squeezed out
from behind closed lids,
freeze rivulets on my cheeks.

Silent as a still life,
a burnished disk
against storm-black horizon,
the sun, just born, appears,
grows more luminous
until a solitary pine,
stark in evergreen robes,
shoots gold light from its spire
and sanctifies the ending of another year.

WALKING BLIND

New Year's Day wakes windless
dank with the scent of promised snow,
hung over with the heavy smell
of cattle corralled close to the log house
which wears wreaths of wood smoke
on its weathered eaves.

The dry earth nudges nostrils
with a mix of crushed sage,
dust, deer droppings,
and far back under the evergreens
the musk of a bull elk's bed
taints cone duff beneath my boots.

Before first light I walk blind,
led onward by sights I sniff,
hints of fragrance found hidden
in angled elbow and bent knee,
the yet unopened gift
of my long bottled desire.

REFUGE

From where I walked yesterday
elk tracks intersect my own
spiraling up the mountainside
encircling aspens
tying up four-wire fences
with blue ribboned trails
over a wrapping of snow.

Following a compass course
they head down for river water,
then wander back, zigzagging,
gnawing beige bark from thick trunks,
working their way up to warmth
that hangs on the ridge like a cloudy quilt.

At night, they curl in cold beds
melting out marks of existence.
I yearn to trail them back
to my own beginnings,
bend my knees, fold my legs,
drop to the fresh fallen snow,
turn in on myself, and sleep.

APRIL ENCOUNTER

Horses crest out of the storm, crusted in white,
briny creatures cast on the shore of morning.

They come roaring like a wave, a flailing rush of hooves
and heads, breaking downhill through a foamy sift of snow.

They snort and blow, whales surfacing from deep night,
the bulk of their bodies black against a sea-silver dawn.

Caught in the sucking undertow of their galloped charge,
I'm deafened by the stillness they surrender in their wake.

Breath rushes out, follows the conch shell curve of my ear,
but all I hear is the shushing sound of my beached heartbeat.

SUNDERANCE

I wondered what could creak
and groan, a moan so wholly human
I searched the frozen trees for sound,
for soul or shadow that unbound
would tell me who was there
invisible in April's early morning air.

I stood stock-still and listened hard,
so hard I heard my breath escape,
a little held-back whispered shush,
the trackless hush of raven's rushing
wings that caught a rising drift of wind
below the ridge's rough and rocky face.

There, again, a pained and weary cry,
a piercing sigh from unseen place,
I tuned my inner ear and heard the hardened
heart of something break. So still,
so sharp and hot, a slant of angled light,
the sun's incomprehensible injury to ice.

A PATCH OF GRASS

Blond bunch grass sticks straight up from the soil's
flaky scalp like a barber's buzz cut.

Split ends crack off under my hand's hard Dutch rub,
letting dried dead hairs drift east on a yellow breeze.

Spurred by last night's spit of scattered snow
pale green growth pushes forth from tender follicles.

Belly down, I stretch out in red dirt and scattered stones
to brush chapped lips against the downy fur of spring.

EARTH INTIMATE

In the mist
stepping with stealth
over wet silver sage
I leave tracks in dampened dust
like the wild one gone before me.

Reaching the rock-edged
spine of the ridge,
I strip in amber light
stacking socks and shoes
sweaty shirt and jeans
and underthings
in a haphazard pile beneath
a wind-beaten bristlecone.

Shale scrapes bare soles
a west wind torments my hair
and in the shifting fog
my chanting splits into
hawk scream and howl.

Running, I soar,
right into the open arms
of morning.

LUNG TA—"WIND HORSE"

Sherpas plant prayer flags on Mount Everest.

Believing the gods disregard elevation
if intent is true enough
I place mine on a hogback ridge above the river

where the wind is wicked,
a brutal bitch of a breeze wearing
angry energy on tattered sleeves.

Arms raised in entreaty, I whisper,

"It is only me, Mother,
come to hold your frantic dancing horse,
kiss your ragged hem, touch your haggard face."

She never stands still long enough to listen.

In her ever holy hurry,
she rears, races away,
trailing a tail of burnt stars.

Undaunted, I scratch words of worship
on bits of lichened black bark
and place them under flat rocks

so they won't blow away.

AN EXERCISE IN OPENNESS

Closed tight as an infant's fist
the fresh-picked bud blushes,
petaled edges barely pink,
the center white as the womb
of the rose from which it grew.

I steady the stem under warm
water, make an angled cut.
A tiny thorn pricks my thumb,
draws blood which runs
a carmine stream down the drain.

Placed in a carved crystal vase
the bloom never knows rain or wind.
Still, each day, it opens a little more
on the sun-puddled countertop
where I rinse and stack dishes.

No memory of earth and air,
no thought of bee or hummingbird,
pollen graces nothing but my nose,
yet it unfolds, pushing back pale petals,
like fingers spreading from a sweaty palm.

VOYEUR

Walking from river to ridge
I watch the day determine herself—
brushing back black bangs,
slipping out of a bed of stars,
rising lazy and slow after long
hours of loving the night.

Glistening wet, various scents waft
from every intimate bend of her body.
Stretching, yawning,
she shifts light and shadow,
settles a soft shawl of clouds
across naked shoulders.

Sipping dew from long-stemmed grass
she eats the last toasted crust of darkness,
steps into her sunrise skirt,
then sits in the hollow of a hill
crossing her elegant legs
to pull on high-heeled boots.

DANCING CLOUD

In the tarnished mirror of Trophy Lake
she flips her salmon-colored skirt,
exposes the pink ruffled rump
and sheer-stockinged legs of another day.

Wind whirled, she kicks high,
shiny heels eclipsing fading stars
as the tight-laced corset of the Tarryall Hills
pushes the pale breast of sun into full view.

Come evening, wearing the limp white lace
of a lazy, hot afternoon, she'll return to twist up
her summer bleached hair, paint her aging face,
spread the thighs of sunset, and turn tricks.

WEED SEED

Floating into my open hand,
the white fluff carries the power
of hoped for rain and rebirth.

Warm under the feathery tickle
my palm tingles, turns wet,
until my smile spreads from lips to eyes
like a shaft of swelling sunlight.

Sheltered by river bank brush,
there is no one to see,
so I flick my tongue to taste
the eons gone into its wispy silk.

Holding the firm stalk,
I kiss the rounded tip,
smooth the dirt beneath,
bury the scattered seeds,

then leave,
knowing I'll return again and again
just to see what grows.

THE FATE OF GRAPES

Graft me to a stanch gnarled stem.
Tie tight the tough vine I'll grow from
with its light green leaves of longing.

Let me hang shriveled in the sun
to darken, mature, sweeten
the sour seeds of unfulfilled desire.

Give me the fate of the finest grapes—
pick, stomp, press— then forsake me
to ferment in the black vat of wanting.

After several seasons return full-hearted
to savor my flavor changed by time,
the alchemy of woman turned to wine.

SLEEPING WITH THE RIVER

Her voice calls me night after night
until finally I go down below her banks
and unroll my bed on the old bridge
that stretches between her shoulders,
to lie quiet and watch the egg-yolk orb
of the moon rise in a cloudless sky.

The jealous wind objects, complaining
through the long light hours, tearing
leaves from the withes of the willow
above my head. Nestled in down,
I am restless, wakened by recurrent
whispers of a lover I will never hold,

the never-ending rush of water over
stone over stone over stone over stone.

THISTLE IN MOONLIGHT

One of the horses gnawed out
the sweet purple flowers
of your prickly heart,
leaving a ray of barbed leaves
spiraling in the silver sage.

Surrounded by vapor
that foreshadows another early frost,
your wan spirit rises
light as down in the night
a helix bound for heaven.

ASTERS

Already, even before late August,
autumn appears, answering
shorter days with longer nights which,
abject at twenty-eight degrees,
leave an acre of yard flowers
curled and blackened by the cold.

Yet, in woods patterned with amber,
at the base of an elder aspen,
green alternate leaves still climb
a single slender stem to a corymb
of six many-rayed lavender asters
whose inner corollas glow gold,
each burning as a separate sun universe.

Anyway you look at it, things die,
whether in season or out of season.
Against all reason some things live,
anchoring themselves in the arrogance
that their time to die just hasn't arrived.

MONOCHROME

White disk, white aura, the sun
tries to shine through fog as rich
as the imagined kiss of the lover
who comes to me in silence
out of the white light of morning.

Though forbidden, one moment
I walk toward him in the glimmered cold;
the next second, I am on my knees,
alone in the autumn snow,
torn by the cries of coyotes.

THE ESTATE OF MY HEART

Bury her alone and apart
on a ridge chastened with wind
with nothing to see but sky.

Promise to return each spring
to see which flowers grow wild
on her unmarked grave:

the full white rose of wanting,
the tulips of a suffering lover,
or narcissus, symbol of the eyes that watch,

waiting for her beloved to appear.

SHADOWS CAST ON SNOW

If stems and seed heads are beautiful,
so too their shadows quivering in the cold,
sketches drawn on the white unmarked morning.

Which to be? Grass bending in the wind
or shadows coming, going,
dependent on ever-changing clouds?

OUTLINE

I trudge through the last storm of the year
writing a boot track message
from log house to ranch gate
across a blank open flat
where the sympathetic wind
coming at night to clean
will scour away loose flakes
and leave snow-packed prints
on gray gravel
the unsteady outline of my leaving.

ROAD WONDERING

Curved rolling ribbons of asphalt,
with frilly thin-stripped borders of grass
laced with yellow wildflowers:

Nothing conjures up completeness
like the unwrapping of black miles
on a summer day where white thunderheads decorate
the buttermilk blue sheetcake of Texas sky.

Why does the road reach out for the things
that continue to escape my active grasp—

Like the change the white-striped line
brings late at night when the world's reduced
to the opalescent spill of headlights,
a watery cascade that washes away
mistakes, errors, and accidents.

Daylight reveals the revolving door of old thoughts,
reviving and engaging my eyes with a heart
still marked with double yellow lines,

the throbbing caution that pulls me
tight into a sweeping curve
then releases me against an unknown horizon.

THE GOAT'S EYELID

"What would happen if one woman
told the truth about her life?
The world would split open."

—Muriel Rukeyser

HOUSEWORK

Housework makes me horny:
all that sucking and blowing,
rubbing and scrubbing,
all that flushing and gushing,
the rushing of water down drains.

Maybe it's the dog hair and dust
that makes me want to get down and dirty,
find the nasty cobwebs hidden
in nooks and cracks and crannies.

All I know is that when it's over
I'm tired, sweaty, breathing hard
and still longing to be kissed.

THE GOAT'S EYELID

I.

Even after all these years I remember his eye,
gold and gloating as he pissed himself
and licked the sticky liquid off his front legs,
then chattered a blat that he believed
the does went for when really all they wanted
was six seconds of sex and his expensive sperm.

He smelled as rank as winter rotted hay
and gave no quarter to anyone who made
their way past his private pen. He glared
with gold eyes, oblong pupils black in the sun,
and lowering his horned head he butted every
mother's child backwards through the fence.

In his sequestered space, I loved and hated him.

II.

Chinese Mongols of the Yiian dynasty
made 'happy rings' from the eye lids of dead goats:
leaving the eyelashes attached they placed the lids
in quick-lime, then carefully steamed and dried them
until they reached the right texture for sexual pleasure.

In the stillness of some 13th century summer night
a man carefully tied a dried eyelid onto his erect penis
so that it tickled and teased his lover during intercourse.
I wonder if the woman, arched and aching inside,
ever gave a thought to the gold eye that gave her sight.

III

I worship memory like some women worship wealth:
at times the buck's scent haunts me as I clean my house,
how after feeding I could never scrub away his smell.
I hear his pleading bleat as the does headed out to graze
and how he stood all day with front feet on a rounded rock,
gold eye gazing, his thin black beard dripping fresh urine,
his long soft eyelashes blinking like a disbeliever.

TENDER SENSIBILITIES

When even the rush of wind
through a raven's wings seems
an explosion to my ears,
I hide my head under a hood
and tie down tender sensibilities
with a rough wool scarf.

Just the thought of them
pierces holes in my heart's
carefully constructed armor
exposing me all over again
to an anguish I cannot answer,
their angry childish cries against
an imperfect, intolerable world.

I admit I've come to hate
the men they are,
but I'll always love the boys
who found ebony feathers
freed from flight and watched
them soar at night in lamp light.

SNIP OF THE SCISSORS

All the men who loved it long are gone.

The first snip of the scissors stabs,
so I close my eyes against the sight
of sun-streaked inches falling
to the cold linoleum floor.

Released from length and weight,
freed from heavy memories of hands,
lips, and breathy whispered words,
the shortened strands lift and curl.

An avenged angel,
I walk out the trailer door
into autumn's moonless night.

Buoyant and alone, I rise,
baptized by a spill of starlight.

SETTLING FOR CRUMBS

Each time they sliced the hot loaves of their love
my mouth watered and I reached out to grab
a thick slab smeared with sweet cream butter
and just-made strawberry jam —

but they had many others to serve,
so I waited, sitting on my hands,
until even the crusty ends were gone.

Then, moistening fingertip with tongue,
I settled for crumbs left on the cutting boards.

THE UNDERSIDE OF THINGS

The afternoon air lay limp, slack
against the inner thigh of early summer,
until a breeze, teasing off the peak,
lifted leaves, skirts, hair, exposing
the secret underside of things.

A woman watered flowers—
delphiniums spiked purple to the sky,
poppies burst open in orange surprise,
peonies, heavy headed, collapsed
into a perfumed jungle of green.

Along that cobbled town street,
the smell of steaks, spilled beer,
a whiff of piss and unwashed arm pit,
incense wafting from a dark shop and
the desiccated dust of no rain in weeks.

Atop a low stone wall of a bridge,
two teenage boys in caps sat cross-legged
above the churning creek, smoking and talking:
"Do you think, like, maybe,
I'm just in love with them all?"

ADDICTION

Ten minutes out of bed on a Sunday
and I struggle with a damn tough decision—

Which tea do I make to erase the tremble
of a night not long enough?

Calming chamomile,
red raspberry leaf that counters female complaint,
Chinese green with its bite of caffeine,
or English Breakfast black that jolts me awake
even when laced with milk?

Not jasmine with its flowery breath
that makes me ache for flesh
or peppermint's sharp slap to the palate.

How do I choose which one to undress,
taking off the paper wrapping,
pulling the tiny string,
holding the tag with tenderness
before dunking into steam?

Which boiling body do I stir with blond honey,
my spoon ringing in the chipped cup
until I drink the sweetness down,
hot in my tight throat?

Which bag will I leave,
wet and limp,
on the stained and cluttered countertop?

BETWEEN STORMS

In the middle of the night I wake
see my face drained and weary in the rain.

Something deep inside me aches
for the intimacy of earth-wise eyes.

I turn to sleep and take all I was ever told
into the making of other dreams.

Outside my window snow makes
a soft hissing sound against the sky.

Geese circle and call across lakes
where the ice is heavy and ready to fall.

Somewhere searing sun bakes the ground,
catches me running hard between storms.

WITHOUT SANCTION

Without sanction, ideas appear
out of a night sky like snowflakes,
to dance and drift, never falling
on silenced tongue, to disappear, absorb,
and be reborn again in a lick of dry lips.
Ungathered, no fingers shape them,
round, hard, deadly as aimed disapproval.
Unwritten thoughts burn like full breasts
within reach of hungry hands, tighten
loin and throat with the knowing
that what I have to give are words,
just words; lined paper, cheap pen,
and black ink that runs wild
only to pool and settle like spent sex,
as muddy and misshapen as snow melt.

TRANSFIGURATION

Truly, I had the patience of a nun
waiting for the resurrection,
but underneath the habit of everyday life,
the black nothingness that said,
"I am no one except a set of hands that serves,"
I was a woman who wanted to wear red panties,
who yearned to stuff my starched white wimple
into an early grave,
dance barefoot in the new turned dirt,
and let my hair grow long again.

Believe me, I prayed, "Please,
let this transformation come
before the rosary beads of wanting
are worn past my day of reckoning."

WHAT HE THOUGHT HE WANTED

I gave him the last of my innocence
even though he never asked,
never held out his hand,
or questioned what a middle-aged married man
would do with such an intense essence.

He held me at arm's length
like a newspaper he could not read,
the expression of angst hanging in his eyes,
reminding me of a time long past
when I first glimpsed my own breasts
unharnessed from the white cotton bra,
the tight annoyance that traveled up from my thighs
and lodged like a lodestone in my throat,
which I tried, again and again, to swallow
while a nameless boy stood tense and trembling.

I never meant to cause him the grief of not knowing
how to hold the fire-hot remnant of the girl I was,
yet I belong to him now, whatever he chooses to do:
stand there cradling his amazement or turn away,
incredulous and ashamed that this,
the one thing he thought he wanted,
is something he doesn't know how to handle.

ANGEL'S SHARE

"A great cognac must be
the expression of the soil."
　　　　—Alexandre Gabriel

My face is as old as the land
and like a great cognac
I am an expression of the soil

gout de terroir
I taste of the earth

eau de vie
I am the water of life

drink from my lips
eat of my heart
pour a little of yourself into me
and I will unfold for you
bouquet wafting until
aromas mixed and blended
we are aged into other identities

and when you depart
the leaving will lift me
an exquisite evaporation
for what I surrender
is only the angel's share.

THE EPICUREAN ART OF
READING A LOVE LETTER

Hungry, eating with my eyes,
I gulp words whole,
swallow sentences,
never pause for periods
or paragraphs, just
inhale the written feast
finding sustenance
in every delicious phrase.

I take a second helping,
slowly savoring ink and paper,
tasting each syllable,
the salt and sweet of sounds,
bitter bits of mixed metaphor,
the separate spice of each simile,
alliance of alliteration and internal rhyme.

Smells and textures measure the meter,
so I chew with great thought,
masticating the meaning of love
taken in tiny bites.

AFTER AN IMAGINARY
AFTERNOON OF LOVING

I wish the light could be more gray,
more soft with sleep and new, instead
of bright and angled slants that show my age,
the dimpled folds of faded skin,
each bruise and liver-shaded spot that marks
where greedy flesh pressed flesh, toasting
the wine-colored taste of late afternoon.

Under breeze-stirred trees I dreamed.
Now a hand, heavy on my hip, keeps
me from rising and dressing; yet the hour calls
me to the company of my other older lover,
the demands that diminish and diffuse
the illicit breeding of illumination
that starves the fruitfulness of awakening.

I will never have a memory of morning,
a drink of dawn, or even one bite of night;
only snatched crumbs of startled intensity
where sun and shadow couple on my closed face,
longing for someone to pick crushed leaves from my fair hair
as I stare into space, to that far away place
past passion, past pain, where lovers are never parted.

INFIDELITY

The names tagged to it never pretend to be pretty
liar, cheater, tramp, harlot, whore, hussy, slut
all those hard-ass sounds determined to pound
a sensitive conscience into submission.

But given a chance to hold hands with intimacy,
it's easy to be disloyal, to leave desperation for desire,
to shut out all outcries except unfaithful endearments
dear one, darling, beautiful, sweet and precious everything.

REMEMBERING TO BREATHE

Before the time I first knew words could breathe,
I never imagined I was visible in any mirror,
visible in a place where life held each facet of being naked
up to an incandescent light which reflected back power
in such an easy way that to this day I feel
each moment I'm alive is an act of violent

behavior, like this art of pushing a pen, these violent
verbs racing headlong across the page, trying their best to breathe,
each inward gasp a cataclysmic feeling,
imperative and important, reflecting back a mirror
image of passion that turns instantly into power,
the way a misbegotten noun announces in a naked

voice, I am all I am ever going to be, a naked
truth, as plain as the color white which in its own stark way is violent
the way purity possesses a singular power
to burgeon into an all-consuming air that breathes
as summer curtains blown against an antique mirror,
so that my mistaking inhaling and exhaling was just a feeling

I'd forgotten, an automatic response lost when feeling
out a conversation late at night, words moving like air, the naked
face of intimacy not yet invented, but imagined in a mirror
of words so well spoken they are invasive, violent,
even extreme acts, so unheard of I forgot how to breathe
for years, and used as an excuse the absence of personal power

that kept me from ever claiming any right to power,
leaving me like a hollow reed bending in the wind, with the feeling
that if I never allowed myself to fully breathe
then I would never perish naked
and alone in some room stuffed with the violent
aftermath of argument, the way calm seas mirror

stormy skies that mirror cold stars that mirror
me, the me held before myself at arms length, too full of power
to ignore, the unyielding and ever violent
temper of loving words that demand a feeling
for something, anything, begging an acceptance of the naked
and unashamed reality of just learning how to breathe

again, so that someday the mirror will show me breathing,
show the holy naked power of accepted flesh,
allow the recognition of feeling that violent lies are just fine.

THE WEEK OF WANTING MORE

"Recklessly
I cast myself away;
Perhaps
A heart in love
Becomes a deep ravine?"

—Izumi Skikibu, 10th Century

THE WEEK OF WANTING MORE

I

Just past dawn, camp stove-hot green tea,
cottonwood leaves, the chortling creek,
talking as if I wanted nothing more than conversation
when really I couldn't get close enough,
couldn't stop reaching out to touch your arm, your face...

So, after the catch-up-chat that follows separation,
we closed the van's double doors and cuddled
on the rough serape spread over your double bed
and let the long weeks of longing heal themselves
with the scent and sound of sex that could not wait.

The after-taste of love teased the morning breeze,
letting us take our ease beneath the trees, sipping
more tea, eating fresh-sliced fruit with yogurt
and granola, laughing at the way we couldn't keep
a working writer's strict schedule if we tried.

II

Yet, later, sprawled in a lawn chair, the cool air
competing with afternoon sun, I read your work.
Silent to the pleas, silent to the scream of old hurts
and the way they warp our lives, silent to the reasons
we forever go on trying to find a way to make love work.

When I'd finished the last page, I saved my thoughts
about repressed anger and editing for another time
and found you stretched out shirtless in the van's
interior shade. I made you hold me hard, sweat-slick
in your arms, until the charm of loving did the trick.

I will not harbor ghosts of hate, but I'll wait forever
if you want me to honor those that made you change,
choice by certain choice, into the man you are today.
There is no way I'll ever let the past encroach on me,
or you, again, my friend, my solace, my buoyant lover.

III

Bourbon and branch water, warmed tortillas wrapped
around tomato, avocado, salsa heavy with cilantro.
A walk along a curving dirt road, the evening alive
with the fragrance of white chokecherry blossoms
and the sound of the stream sighing over exposed stones.

Alone in camp you teased me with a spring-form tea ball,
turning it into a wise-mouth character who didn't give a flip
about being a short, wire-mesh steel kinda guy without a penis.
I laughed until I was sick, my stomach hurt, and I cried real tears
because he was so desperate for affection, begging for a French kiss.

Weary of wandering through interlocking circles of conversation,
we washed by the creek, then crawled quiet into the rumpled bed,
all the words we'd been waiting for finally spoken, finally said.
We snuggled silent, content, while the sun sank part way into tomorrow
and we soothed and stroked and touched and tasted until we slept.

IV

But the words returned around midnight when there wasn't any light
except for the glisten of stars through the breeze-stirred leaves.
We murmured memories of earlier times when the van sheltered
us from sun, from storms, from prying eyes, and sighing confessed
that the closeness we craved was at long last being met and satisfied.

Homemade bread with honey and almond butter, the licking of sticky
fingers as we ate, sharing more stories, sharing jasmine tea, sharing
the returned sun that marked one day down and six to go. I know
I shouldn't count, I said, but the magic makes me anxious for it all,
for every minute I can savor, seclude and save for future days away.

A private concert: you, your guitar, five new songs. Seeing myself
the mirror of your inspiration, the reflection of you loving me,
made me smile the entire time you sang. When an ordinary woman
becomes goodness incarnate, becomes goddess and giver of life, then
all things surrounding her shimmer with laughter and joy and light.

V

Driving away in the middle of the day was difficult. Disliking enforced
separation, I mothered up to the back of the van like a calf following a cow,
my jeep weaving the white lines right behind you, maneuvering around RVs,
climbing the pass, construction stops wearing my patience, the rain slowing
us down as we pulled into town and stopped at MacDonald's to reconnect.

I don't eat junk food, but the grilled chicken sandwich and Coke we shared
dared me not to protest too much because here I could hold your hand, or rest
my fingers on your inner thigh and lie about the way I was tough enough to get by
without you, didn't need the sound of your breathing in my ear, the near beating
of your heart, the dear laughter that comes after we collapse, in time, together.

I worried about the rented house and whether it was right to play at being married,
until you carried in our bags and eyed the overstuffed couches, the straight-backed
dining room chairs, the stairs that led up into a heaven of sunlit bedrooms, and
best of all, the tall-sided clawfoot tub, and a kitchen complete with pots and pans
so you could cook and I could clean up in-between our bouts of making love.

VI

Safeway played golden oldies on the speakers as you danced me down the aisles,
the red plastic basket bumping my butt as other women stared and smiled and
wished their husbands would be just as wild about grocery shopping. What did
we buy? Lettuce, carrots, tomatoes, avocados, olive oil, small red potatoes, Asiago,
green onions, plums, and two rib-eye steaks, enough to make an anniversary meal.

On our return we walked the wide side streets and stretched cramped, tired muscles,
the odd complaint that a delicious heaviness hung about us like a gathering storm
accompanied every step until we met up with ourselves again outside the door.
We sipped a bit of bourbon in the late afternoon light as you stroked back my hair,
swearing sweetly that nothing in sixty years had prepared you for a woman like me.

Within seconds I was blouseless and cradled against your chest, the rest remains
a blur of sharply focused snap shots one following quickly on the other—me going
half naked up the stairs when your hand reached for the top of my shorts and pulled
me down onto the rough carpeted steps, my hands pushing against the narrow walls,
the world wheeling swiftly above me in a series of white wood banisters and railings.

VII

We laughed and made it up two more steps before you kissed me again, the trail
to our intended shower lost in the dancing slatted shadows of sun through blinds.
I didn't mind in the least: the pebbled rug like little stones beneath, the brisk breeze
that teased the sweat on my skin, the sound of traffic outside like the sea rushing
against some exotic shore where surely we would come, shipwrecked, to rest.

But then, the top of the landing and I could not walk. My legs went out from under
me and I was down, sinking into oblivion, the waves of nips and kisses pulling at me,
dragging me beneath the surface of sensation until I was gone, gasping for air,
flailing, trying not to go to the deepest dark even as the light receded and I believed
with certainty that I was dying and would never be able to come back to you.

When I woke, huddled against the wall like an addict on the other side of her latest fix,
I was shaking hard, the floor trembling, every sound as sharp as a shot, every bit
of light stabbing my eyes, the taste of blood bitter on my tongue, and you bringing
me a wet cloth to cool the fever that burned beneath my skin, you carrying me into
the shower and washing my face and arms and back and breasts and legs and hair.

VIII

Candlelight. A small wild rose picked from the side-yard. Evening breeze stealing
through the open windows as we ate and drank Badger Mountain cabernet, crystal
glasses winking back the light. We took our mug of herbal tea and chocolate chip
walnut cookies onto the front steps where I sat below you, between your knees,
the serape over your shoulders cocooning us in comfort as we counted brightening stars.

I wonder where we are? I asked. This didn't seem like heaven. This didn't seem
like home. This seemed like something out of drink or dream or desperation coupled
with delirious joy. We sat and listened to the night sounds of town life: music
in the park, children playing, cars shushing past, until, at last, it got too cool to stay
and you took my hand and led me past the undone dishes, kissing me up the stairs to bed.

I remember waking when you woke to sit bolt upright on the edge of the bed. Okay?
I asked and you said, lie down, go back to sleep, and I heard you creep soft across
the room, drink from the water glass on the shelf, and go into the bathroom. It was sultry,
the night stifled with rain that couldn't fall, with clouds crushed in against the peaks.
You read my mind, opened the window, curled against my back and whispered "beauty."

IX

We agreed to pace ourselves and not let lust misappropriate the trust we had in love;
and yet again at dawn you had me down in the tangled web of sheets, my sleepy eyes
barely awake as I urged you on, crying take me, take me again and again. Have you
ever wondered about the things in this world that love tries to mend? I have. It seems
that life is forever pulling apart, rending and tearing, while love, love, does the repairing.

Walking clean streets where sprinklers sput-sputted their arcs of water into rainbows,
we talked and talked and laughed and kissed like customers too long on the lonely list.
We drank our tea by candlelight and ate the omelet made with mushrooms, onions,
eggs and cheese. Wheat toast drizzled with honey was serving as dessert when one gold
drop lingering on your lip caused me to tip my plate while reaching for it with my tongue.

I pushed the dishes aside, clearing a spot before you and sat straddling your shoulders.
I couldn't have been any bolder if I tried, but you didn't seem to mind as you succumbed
to my kiss and then administered, with adept authority, a post-breakfast breast rub, pink
nipples peeking out from under the shoved-up shirt and bra, the awe making my skin
crawl beneath the tender tracks your fingers made across the landscape of my damp lap.

X

Don't say the table won't hold us, it will. Don't worry about cold wood, the stains,
the spills. Just kiss me here, here. Unpin my hair. Toss the clothes whichever way
they'll go and show me here, there, with teeth and tongue and lips the magic of my hips
moving in time with your words. Coax me. Convince me. Encourage me. Enchant me.
Enthrall me until the walls echo with my choking cry, don't stop, don't stop, don't....

I won't, you whisper, holding me wet and shaking beneath the chandelier, I'm here,
I'm here. I won't leave. I know how much you need. Hush now, catch your breath,
catch your breath. Do you know how beautiful you look stretched out on the table with
the sunlight streaming in your hair? Yes, yes, of course I care. I love you like I've never
loved before, and more, much more than I have the words to say. I'm here. I'm here.

It's okay, I say, I'm fine. No, you didn't hurt me. It's the pleasure bordering on the pain.
It takes awhile to regain my composure. Composure? We laugh until the tears begin again
and I beg you to switch places as I unzip your jeans and push them to the floor. More?
you ask. *Mas y mas*, I quip and bite the guilty lower lip that held the honey. Give me just
one reason why we should quit now when the day is just beginning to be hot and funny.

XI

I shake out the serape and spread it like an altar cloth upon the table and guide you victim
to a priestess who is willing to sacrifice the only thing she treasures for the sake of love.
I slip the rose from its tumbler vase and brush it across your closed eyes, bearded face,
your neck and chin. I dance it round and round your ears, across your chest and groin,
leaving pink petals in my wake where they stick like miniature pins to your sweaty skin.

Breathless now, rise, opening your eyes in anticipation of an expected treat, my tongue
tasting the rounded length of you, the beat of hearts racing toward an unseen goal until
I stop before you reach the peak of exploding like a fallen star. I climb up on a chair,
crawl on hands and knees to sit astride your lap and stare you sweetly in the eyes to chide
don't wait a minute longer as my hips pull out, push in, stronger, stronger, stronger.

I'm so weak I can hardly roll to the side as we laugh about what would have happened
if the craftsman who built the table hadn't done a good job. How would we explain
the shatter of wood and splinters in the middle of the floor. No more, no more, I say,
it hurts to laugh this way. Stop. Stop. Let me up. Let me mop up this mess and dress.
Let me do the dishes and sweep the floor. Let me catch my breath again and go outdoors.

XII

No, you say, just rest and I will do my best to calm you, comfort you. I'll draw a bath
and we can soak ourselves until we turn to soggy prunes. I slept, woke to water running
in the tub, the dishes cleared, the smear of sex drying on my legs. You came with open
arms and scooped me up, serape and all. Even dust motes danced to music only I could
hear as you stood me before the mirror to look at us blushed, bedecked with petals.

The water rushed the overflow as we settled into place, your face against my hair, my head
tucked into your shoulder, back against chest, your hands cupping my breasts, your legs
around my thighs. And the quiet gurgling contained us, soothed us, restrained us, kept
us from moving in the closet-like space, no place to twist or turn or get into trouble, only
minuscule bubbles burbled from our flesh and buoyed the bits of floating rosebud.

We whispered. Why? I don't know, there was no one to hear, though we heard music
cascading in from the street. We were weary, wanting rest and yet the water stirred you
to prod me from the back and I had no lack of luck, of trust, of desire, nothing to keep me
from rolling and crouching above your loins like a lioness at a kill: the taste sweet
with soap as you flinched from being sore, but I could not set you free, let you be.

XIII

Who said love was meant for the young? I came unstrung in the splash of water
against my rump and cried out a kind of agony known only in the war against self.
You held me until I quit shivering, then washed me well, the oatmeal smell of soap sliding
over the swells of hip and breasts. You would not let me return the favor, saying you'd
rather savor the sight of me standing there dripping on the floor, eyes begging for more.

We toweled each other off with brisk and frisky ease, then sprinted up the stairs to rest,
yes, rest, a thirty minute sleep to keep us from forgetting we had other things to do besides
make love all day. We dressed, then drove the winding miles to another mountain town,
listening to music, pointing out places to take pictures, saying we wished we lived here all
the time, wanting that same time to stand still and never move, to keep us together.

The shops held nothing that we needed, just a chance to walk, to browse, and voice out
loud our thoughts about cookware, awful art work, quirky clothes, and desired books.
We took time to stop and have Chai tea and split a chocolate almond croissant, crumbs
scattered where we sat outside in the spangled air of recent rain, where we watched
people drifting past and wondered if any of them had once loved the way we loved.

XIV

Safeway held no secrets. We only needed one avocado to complete our supper menu
and some bananas for our breakfast. But still you danced me past the bread and chips,
our hips swaying to the tunes that echoed through the room. You made me laugh, made
me glad the other women lusted, the mother of a toddler smiling in the aisle, a teenager
pointing to a friend, the cashier's flirting eyes. I tried, but could not hide, my loving you.

We behaved. We sat and drank our bourbon without ice and sprawled together cuddled on
the couch. You sang a song you wrote for me and taught me how to speak some lines
in harmony. Somehow the talk turned to home and far away troubles, the fear of not
knowing what to do. It's not you, you soothed and stroked my hair from my face and
placed your hand against my heart: true, good, kind, loving. Shhh, it isn't you.

A salad, soup with corn, beans and chile, tortillas toasted brown and rolled with cheese.
We sipped wine and ate like survivors from a storm until every single crumb was gone.
We took tea and sat upon the stoop and watched the world go by in its quiet humble way
and neither of us had much to say. We sat and looked and listened with eager ears
to everything there was and everything that wasn't yet alive in the balmy evening air.

XV

No mas, querida. Okay, I said, and shooed you up to bed so I could clean the kitchen
and regroup my thoughts. Already showered, smiling, relaxing on the bed you read
an herb farm cookbook when I walked into the room. I washed my face, brushed my hair,
slipped on a satin gown so not to tempt the gods who might look at us and frown at
indiscretion. I picked a couple of poems I loved and read out loud to share the sounds.

I didn't do a thing but stretch a leg straight and you were there kissing me above the knee,
nibbles gliding up my inner thigh, and poor Blake, poor Graves, poor Shakespeare were
forgotten, the book dropped to the floor, my fingers twined in graying hair as you parted
me and tasted me wet and wanting you again. What demon is this that dares us to care
to the point of exhaustion, that dares us to return again and again before we finally sleep?

"No wonder of it, sheer plod makes plough down sillion shine and blue bleak embers fall,
gall themselves, and gash gold vermilion." Hopkins wakes me, the sun sneaks through
a crack in the blinds. I find your back and kiss you until you wake, take me in your arms.
Morning, beauty, did you sleep? I did, and you? Like the dead and I don't want to move.
Go without me on your walk and I'll have tea and toast waiting for you when you return.

XVI

I never seem to learn the lessons I needed most in life, the ones that keep us from hurting
ourselves, from straying from the traveled path, from stumbling, falling, galling ourselves.
I walked, then jogged the asphalt streets and felt the day's heat already starting to burn.
I missed you beside me, missed you matching me step for step, missed you teasing me,
so I took short cuts, hurried back, rounded the last corner and smiling, waved and ran.

Leaning against the open door, playing the mandolin, you stood in baggy trousers with no
shirt or shoes, your delight written in your eyes as you handed me a cup to sip.
Not minding my sweat or smell, you snuggled me close on the couch and talked as if
I'd been gone a week. *No mas, querido,* I said, as your hand drifted between my legs.
We must eat, wash and dress, then pack and clean. It's time to leave this little house.

Bowls of fruit, pieces of toast and we talked, the candle burning away the minutes,
until I told you I wanted to bathe alone, be alone, and find some time to grieve alone.
You honored my request, left to shower on your own, pack your things, but you could
not stay away, you brought me towels and soap, checked to see if I had hot water.
Covering myself with white wash cloths, I shooed you away, smiling like a spoiled child.

XVII

Closing the door on those three days wasn't easy, but we convinced ourselves that the four yet to come could be better. We'd be back in the public eye and would have to try to be discreet, a word that didn't slip easily on either of our tongues. We drove downtown and parked and walked and looked at books and bought some cards and tried on hats and sat on the patio of a place that served us sandwiches and iced-tea beneath umbrella shade.

You set the rules, then break them, I scolded, as you leaned across and kissed me. Those women are watching. I know, you said licking mayonnaise from your lips with a wicked twist of tongue. Maybe they'll learn something. I laughed and smacked away the hand reaching for my knee. Please, I said, we have a job to do and you're the one who said let's be professional. Excusing yourself politely, you left me sitting silent in the sun.

Returning with a chocolate mousse, one spoon, and two macaroons, you said, allow me, and fed me bite by bite, inciting others who were close enough to see delight beaming in my eyes. You're incorrigible, I said. I know, you answered, and kept it up until the bowl was scraped and every crumb finger-lipped from the plate into my mouth. Okay? you asked. *Querido, mi amor*, I adore you, but *no mas. Comprende? No mas.*

XVIII

You fussed about the college dorm and flirted with the conference receptionist until you'd ousted any roommate and had a room alone right next to me, even though I shared mine with a friend. We were faculty and every single propriety had to be met if we were going to be trusted and believed. I was prepared to be sequestered and deprived of your company. I was willing to be cool and tight-lipped, but light-hearted. I was ready to be parted.

We drove to dinner with my friend and found a booth tucked in a corner where no one could see and ate Caesar salads with chicken and drank Chardonney and there was nothing I could say to convince you that anything at all had changed. Come to me, you whispered when we left, be with me. Let's find a way. It's okay. We'll be quiet and unassuming, we'll just resume where we left off. I need you near me. I need you now.

I took my running shorts and shoes, a tube of lipstick and my toothbrush. You'd left the door unlocked so I checked the outer hallway and slipped inside your room, giggling like a girl going to a slumber party. You waltzed me in a circle and showed me the twin mattresses together on the floor, then you locked the door, and turned out the lights, undressed me and laid me down in the darkness, hearts beating in time, together.

XIX

At dawn we left separately then met in the parking lot to walk the streets and talk. I never knew I could laugh so much. How do you do that to me? It's easy, you said, I just talk and you think I'm funny. I never knew I had such desire, so much passion. How do you do that to me? It's easy, you said, I just touch you and you respond and your pleasure is my pleasure and I'm honored to be part of the process, proud you allow me love you.

What will happen to us? Nothing bad can come of this. We're fine. We're here now, loving each other. It's enough. We're blessed. Be grateful and forget the rest. We'll find our way. We'll be okay. Somehow everything will work out. The gods are good to those who love, to those who invest their hearts and care. You believe me, don't you. Yes, its only that sometimes the fear comes creeping in and decides to stay. We'll be okay.

By late afternoon classes were over, a rose saved from the side of the yard had wilted in its makeshift plastic bottle vase in the jeep. I took a salvaged plum back to my room and when I walked by room 118 your door opened and you pulled me inside saying, I think you need a nap, some time to rest, recuperate before we go back out to join the others. What's sequestered in your hand? I placed the plum in your outstretched palm.

XX

Rubbing my back with scented lotion, any notion that we had of rest fled as we touched and kissed half-dressed on the makeshift bed. If this is resting then I believe we've failed the test, I said. Okay, we'll sleep, you said pulling the blinds tight to shut out the light. I felt you near me on your knees, heard the sound of you biting into something soft, felt the first sweet drop plop between my breasts. What? I asked. The plum, you answered.

Bite by bite you ate and squeezed the juice from pome to skin, then licked me clean, the sticky after burn making me yearn once more for you. You circled lips and nipples, navel and thighs until I writhed upon the bed, slid the fruit half-eaten between my legs where wet met wet and cool met warm and in the gathering storm of contracting muscles I called for you and you were there, inside, calm in the center of whirling squall.

And then, we slept. I don't know why I wept within my dream or woke feeling clammy and unclean, but you seemed to know exactly what I needed as you helped me rise, took my hand, led me to the shower and lathered me with soap. I couldn't tell if what I felt was hopefulness or hopelessness. I only knew that when the water dripped from your lips to mine it was time to curb the wanting, to rein us in and stop the daunting fear of being hurt.

XXI

I wore blue. A swirling skirt and chambray shirt, a cowgirl hat and boots. The dude
ranch dinner was a silly, carefree hoot. Bbq beef and beans, cornbread, corn-on-the-cob,
slaws and salads. Corona beer and cowboy music blasting from the band. We sat too
close and teased each other with our table-hidden knees. Offering up your hands,
remnants of red sauce around the nails, you asked, is sucking fingers acceptable?

I laughed and hissed, go away, you make me crazy. Go away before I'm in your lap,
my skirt hiked up around my waist. No, I don't want a chocolate cookie. Go away...
but as you took your plate and left, I wanted to yell, come back, come back, stay
with me and let the others say what they will. We'll allow ourselves some latitude for
shift and change, arrange our wanting so it evens out, eases into acceptable behavior.

The crowd clapped and I was there sitting on a ring of stones, alone, listening to you sing
and play, the music working magic as the last of day gave over to the night. I had no right
to claim you inside my head, but I did. I watched you sway and move, the guitar cradled
like a lover in your arms. I heard your words and felt the beat and swore that you were
mine, that I could have you anytime if I just asked, *mas, por favor, mas y mas, mi amor.*

XXII

Driving one-handed down the winding road through darkness, your other hand rested on
my leg. Friends joked in the back and we were happy to be hidden away from other eyes.
We didn't need the gory scene encountered in the sprinkling rain, the wipers swishing back
the surprise of a truck stopped dead, its hood wrinkled back to the windshield, a black cow
hit, but still alive, her insides spilled across the lanes. I felt her pain, begged for a gun.

Hush, *Luz*, there's nothing we can do, but drive on through, let the police take care of it.
There are people, too, and I know they're hurt, somewhere out there in the dirt and rain.
We'll just be in the way. Already others have stopped to help. The traffic tangled up along
the edges of the road and we wound our way through and traveled on, the laughter stilled,
the magic gone. You reached up, wiped my cheek with your thumb, then held my hand.

The band was going to jam, so you played again as I sat curled up on a couch and watched
you weave the magic back with melody and rhyme. The night grew late, but when you
left I waited while the others sang and saw your back go out the door, the guitar case
swinging by your side. I made myself stay until my yawns became too obvious. I gave
away my seat, said good-night, tip-toed up the empty halls to your unlocked door.

XXIII

What happened then? Something had changed in your approach. Nothing silent and sweet as I was used to, but something bold and demanding, your hands everywhere at once, your voice hard in my ear, urging me, pushing me, shoving me further and further into an act of passion, and every time you asked, I answered yes, yes, I guess it was the violence on the road, how quickly we can be smashed apart, love and life snatched so fast away.

When you finally took your turn I had burned down into embers, glowing hot inside, but flaking away like charcoal and ash, my limbs splayed, my skin going gray in the wan light seeping silver through the blinds. You were there moving slow, saying spread your legs wider, take me in, take me all, take me, love me, love me, hold me, god hold me, then you couldn't stop, the waves of pleasure twisting to pain and you were crying out in Spanish:

No more, no more. *Madre, no mas.* You were gone where I couldn't find you, couldn't reach you no matter how I smoothed and soothed your skin beneath my sweating hands. Don't go away, I whispered as you shook and trembled, the face in front of mine not resembling the man I knew and loved. Come back, oh my god, come back to me. But you were gone into another place, back to a time that tortured you as I watched.

XXIV

Helpless to your pleas for help, I cried and kissed your grimaced face, your eyes open but unseeing, speaking not to me but to men who had you cornered in the smoke and dust. Your body burned, a fever raging beyond the realm of sex. Something fetid filled the room. Lie back, I said, catch your breath. But you fought, fists clenched, your jaw clamped against the fierce and hate-filled words that whispered forth between your moans.

I kept calling for you to return, but you could not hear over the horses wheeling, reeling in the fire fight. *Agua,* you croaked, *agua,* and I tried to rise to get the glass and quench your thirst, but you wouldn't let me go, you clutched me close, your fingers buried in my naked flesh and said, don't leave, don't leave, *querida* don't leave me while I'm dying. I was crying because I believed it true, that I'd never have you back beside me whole.

It must have been my weeping that pulled you back from vision into being, seeing again the dorm room walls, hearing voices laughing in the halls, because you pushed me back to stare, then gathered me to your chest, our hearts pounding breast to breast, as you said hoarsely, I didn't hurt you, did I? Tell me I never hurt you. No, no, I'm okay. Talk to me. Can you tell me where you went? What sent you over that bitter edge?

XXV

What was that? you asked. Not sure, I said. Vision, waking dream, flashback.
Something triggered by our savage need. There was dust and smoke, so thick, so dry
I couldn't breath. I had no shoes. Someone brought me a dead man's boots, black and up
to my knees. I fought hard to reach you, get back to you, but I was spinning through
space, cart-wheeling around, but you were there just beyond the grasp of my hand.

Was it the writing? Putting it down on the page that made the rage return. I don't know,
but I'm never going back there again. It's over and done with. Do you hear me.
Yes, I understand. You get to choose, you never lose yourself without a choice.
You have a voice in this. You decide what memories to discard or savor and save.
It's okay I'm here, I care. Let's not talk about it anymore. Let it go back to its grave.

This time I took you by the hand and led you to the tub and as I rubbed your body,
lean and hard with years of work, I prayed for light to supersede the lurking shadows,
for help and healing of the hurt. I laid you down, kissed your face, spread the sheet
over our nakedness, and held you as a mother holds her child. In just a little while
you were asleep, but I stayed wakeful, watching as the hours passed to keep you safe.

XXVI

At dawn you were ready to walk out into the world. You'd slept like someone cured
of acute disease. I dragged behind as we strolled the streets, everything in me tired
and uncertain, fearful of that too-thin curtain between the worlds of past and present.
You said you remembered but brushed it off, saying it wasn't worth talking about, and
after classes and a needed rest we'd take our friends out for a steak and celebrate.

The afternoon was hot and muggy, without much breeze to stir up a storm so it would rain.
Cloud cover came and I thought it would be the perfect light for photographs. We took
a chance and wandered across an unmown field where the grass was high and a rail fence
served as a spot to lean. Dressed with blue on blue, work shirt, Levi's, boots and hat,
you looked so handsome, fresh, and new that I found myself falling in love with you.

I had you sit, then stand, lie in the wildflowers, your guitar propped against your leg,
and it took every bit of will for me not to beg you to undress and take me there in the dirt
and thistles, the sun obscured by passing clouds. I wanted the wind to lick my skin. I
wanted us to sing the opening lines of a song we knew so well. Reading my mind you
asked, want to do it again, and I grinned behind the camera lens and kept on shooting.

XXVII

Why is waiting the hardest part of loving? There was no time for us to breathe together,
none-the-less tempt and tease with so many other people close around. I had trouble just
thinking about the night to come and how I could get to you and be alone. So by the time
I dressed up in denim skirt and skimpy top, I was wound up tighter than a watch's spring,
ready to unwind at the slightest thing that would tip the world, slide you to my side.

Our friends urged caution, but I rebelled against the rules and flirted like a unschooled girl.
I ate off your plate and drank your wine and didn't even mind the looks that came our way
when I kissed you between courses. I laughed, swung my hair, flirted with your friends
and said I didn't care and could we order cheesecake and share, one fork, four mouths,
passing white bites dripping strawberries back and forth across the narrow table.

I was being brassy, sassy with that kind of crazy attitude that says the world can do
whatever it wants, but I'm breaking free, I want to run wild, I want to have fun. I laughed
more that night than I ever have before. I wanted more and more and more. I wanted
to even up the score and balance heartache with happiness. I wanted another chance to take
you to the makeshift bed and love you until we both came undone, until the sun rose again.

XXVIII

The others went their separate ways—some to watch the rodeo, some to drive and park
beside the road. You took me back to change so we could walk our dinner off and
adjust our attitude. I wasn't in the mood for something calm and nice, but you talked
me into going and I was glad you took me to the park to swing on swings and climb
monkey bars, and stroll around the lake, taking time to stop and kiss and reminiscence.

It wasn't very late when we headed back thinking we'd have a chance to just vegetate and
sit and watch the sun go down behind the peaks. But we passed our friend out in the hall
and something in her eyes told me to take her off alone and hold her in my arms as she
cried, it isn't fair, I shouldn't have to choose. Why does someone have to lose when
all I want to do is love them both. I want to care and be there and make it right for him.

Tears pooled then trickled down her chin and I let her cry within my safe embrace. It's
okay, whatever it is, it's okay, you'll be all right. We're here for you and will do anything
you need for us to help you out. I know you doubt the truth of what it means to love and
no it isn't fair, but life never is, and when you make your choice make it for the sake of
your heart and let the others find their way. You have no say in how they'll think or feel.

XXIX

They walked into the night and we found ourselves sequestered in your room where the
last of dusk cast a gloomy gray aura off the walls. We'd just begun to talk and kiss when
we heard movement in the hall and you hushed me. Someone tapped at the door and when
we didn't answer walked on past. You looked out through the peephole and said, it's her,
you must go help her if you can. I hated that I had to choose between the two of you.

We talked. I understood how she could want so many men at once: one waiting at home,
an old lover who walked away and now waited for her in the night, the new friend she
phoned each day, the one who didn't want her to stray from the passion they'd found.
Why is life forever bound by the things we want, the things we need, by romance and
intensity? Love shouldn't be this hard, as uncertain as the last card you're dealt.

I felt her pain, her indecision, her self-derision that she couldn't keep it simple. He's
worried about you, I said. What shall I tell him? I'll come with you, explain how
difficult it is to be committed to one man. Here, I said, hold my hand. I want to warn you
that it's more dangerous going back than moving forward. The unknown is safer territory
than trying to unearth the seeds you've already sown which have grown into weeds.

XXX

Your door swung open on its noisy hinge. The room was dark and in the stark light
spilling from the bathroom I saw you lying on the mattress on the floor. She went right
into your open arms and nestled on your chest crying like a child who hurts the worst
because of fear. I drew near, settled on your other side and took her pain as my own.
You reassured us, held us close, let whatever wisdom you had gleaned settle on our hearts.

I let her have the half of you she needed most. I let us coast there in the circle of your
smile as your fingers traced patterns on our arms, pulled the hair away from our faces
as she choked out the tangle of how she had loved your friend but couldn't go back to him.
You let me wail without words, patting my back, letting me withdraw to a place where the
pace of pain wouldn't be so hard to take. Then, we laughed, gasping for each breath.

This is the way, you said, that porno films begin. Two women and a man, broken hearts
and no one knowing where to turn. We slapped your stomach, tried to pull away,
but your tightening arms urged us to stay, the comic relief the perfect medicine for grief.
When our breathing calmed, she took her leave, thanked you for keeping us blessed,
then confessed she was going back to her own room alone, to wash, then read, then sleep.

XXXI

You wanted me in a way I'd never known, but I was iced beyond my bones and shivered
standing there. You kissed my hair, but I could not be reached. I cannot, I said
and hurt you by refusing to meet your need. Just tell me what to do, you said. And I
answered, just hold me, nothing more, just hold me until I sleep. You undressed and
laid me down still in my shorts and shirt, still trembling from the aftermath of tears.

We'd never spent a night together without making love. It confused you and when
you woke to close the window against the cold I could tell you had pulled into yourself.
I snuggled the broad warm shelf of your back but you flinched, pushed us apart.
I knew your heart was comprised. How do we keep things on an even keel, find the real
and lasting center that will keep the waves from washing us under and we drown?

I did not sleep. I lay awake wondering what kind of love it takes to make our hearts
stay active and alive. I wanted nothing more than to be beneath you once again, do any
thing it took to help us mend. I lay listening to you breathe, wondering what you dreamed.
I lay wanting so much more than what had happened to make us drift apart. I kept from
crying by telling myself morning would make it better, morning will mean another start.

XXXII

Even before dawn we were both awake, trying to make some sense of what had happened.
But we didn't know. We tried to talk but words kept getting in our way. You can't love
them all, you said. You can't take on everyone's pain and stay alive. You left me for her.
You told me too. I know, but I didn't think you'd go. We came back to you. I understand,
but I didn't want all that between my stupid hands not knowing what to do.

Will you walk with me? Not today. Go on your way. Go alone. Take some time for
perspective and I'll stay here and try to get more sleep. I wanted to kiss you back into
loving me, wanted to erase every little trace of the place where we'd stumbled in the night,
fumbled our way out of love and couldn't find the right way to get back in love again.
I left you lying on your side. Your breathing deep to keep my uncertain hands at bay.

I ran like the world itself was in pursuit, my feet pounding the pavement until I couldn't
breathe. A cold and dampish wind rustled through the leaves. And when the lights
came on in a car parked in a deserted lot, the thought rushed through my mind that some
one might catch me and leave me on the road half-dead. My leaden legs refused to move
faster as I shoved the thought away, thought instead of you lying warm and safe in bed.

XXXIII

The day trudged on. You wouldn't meet my eye no matter how I tried to let you know I
was still there, still cared, still ached with longing for some sort laughter, some hint
of song. Who was wrong? Did we know what happened? Like a teenager in danger
of giving up secrets to the rest of the class, I scribbled a note on a torn piece of paper
and passed it up the aisle. You read it. Smiled. Then turned to listen to our speaker.

There is nothing weaker than a woman who is certain she's ruined everything just by
being who she is. I couldn't figure out why confessing my own need for comfort
should interfere with yours for wanting something more. Certainly there was time and
space for all we needed from each other. I asked you to my class and you came to talk
about your songs, all the wrong turns you'd made and how you found your way back.

A TV crew caught me as I left and wanted an interview out on the lawn. I looked
for you but you were gone, but as I stood before the camera answering questions
I saw you across the quadrangle sitting on your windowsill, bare feet bouncing
off the brick wall, head bare to the breeze. When I was finished I kicked off my heels
and ran the distance between us, arriving breathless into the circle of your open arms.

XXXIV

Let's go eat, you said. Meet me in front and we'll find a quiet corner where we can talk.
I couldn't walk fast enough to the other side of the building though I wilted in the heat.
Every question I asked you batted away, saying wait, time enough for that. We sat
in our favorite booth—ordered a bowl of gumbo and a glass of wine, a pesto chicken
sandwich with a tonic and lime. Then you talked and wouldn't let me interrupt.

What happened was just a glitch, a bitch of a night, a bitch of a morning, but then without
warning you sent your note and melted my reserve away. What can I say except I claim
the fault as mine. I felt insufficient, ill-at-ease, with no way of showing how much I
cared without seizing you and loving all the hurt away. Not yet, let me finish. I love you
more than any man has a right to love and you'll have to help me know how I need to be.

There's nothing to be sorry for, but this—that in loving we come so close to sheer
perfection we cannot abide even a slight deflection of our ardor. But love goes out with
a mind of her own, adrift to lift and bless, to sanctify no less even the smallest reason
that we care. We do love a disservice if we turn away from those in need, even if they bleed
and leave us damaged by their sorrow. If we love today, then tomorrow we are saved.

XXXV

I ate your rice. You ate my slaw. We sat with thighs pressed tight. When our friends
arrived you waved them away with a gesture. My need for you is like the air I breathe,
I cannot see or hear or even stand without you near. I don't know how to act when I've
never felt this way before. Can you forgive me for being such a jerk, a boob, an idiot
who only wants your love and to love you in return? Can I learn how to do this right?

I didn't want to laugh, but I did. Beating yourself up in front of me made me love you
even more. Of course I couldn't guffaw, but I saw your vulnerability and kissed your
palm and held it to my heart beneath my breast and said, taking responsibility for our own
actions is the beginning of believing we can accomplish anything at all. I forgive you,
and for my part I'm sorry too and wish we could just undo it and forget.

Let's get out of here, you said. We wadded up our napkins and walked across the parking
lot to pick up the film we'd dropped off the day before. And there you were, captured
on that sparkled afternoon when everything had been so perfect-tuned it made our ears
hurt. We flipped through photos, laughing, sighing, asking again how we got off track.
Dried rose petals stirred in the jeep's front seat when you opened the passenger door.

XXXVI

That night we dressed for a book signing and a concert. Somehow we ended up looking
like we'd chosen matching clothes, blues and browns and beiges supported by heeled
boots and hats. We had to act aloof, like we didn't know each other because bigwigs
and studio executives were everywhere. You played and sang to great applause, I
read poetry to the same, and in passing we laughed and smiled at the game we played.

I danced with other men, you sang backup for the other bands, but somehow we found
stolen moments to connect. You caught me coming back from the ladies room and hinted
we should meet out back beside the van and try to have a little time all to ourselves. Last
night together; and one more half day before the fates would drift us home to our mates.
I took the easy out, turned around, crept out through the darkened lot and found you there.

We stripped off boots and hats, but kept our clothing on and just snuggled on the bed
content to talk and touch. We didn't even kiss. We kept our missing under control and let
our words caress and soothe our souls. After all these days of contact, all the nights
entwined, we wanted so much more than what we'd gotten, our little housekeeping time
long forgotten, the future weeks and months apart stretching before us like a lonely yawn.

XXXVII

You held me, captive in your van, and whispered that you wanted me again and would
I come and stay with you, sleep with you, make love to you. Yes, I answered, yes,
and yes. Forgetful of the risk. Forgetful of the hurt. I promised myself to your
warm embrace, laced up my skirt, pulled on my boots and left you lying with starlight
in your silver hair. Closing the door I heard you say, I want you more than ever before.

The music done, equipment put away, people strayed to their cars and left. We said our
good-byes and went our separate ways, promising to meet beneath the dorms to jam. But
we had other plans and you reassured me that you didn't mind missing all the parties and
the fun. I just want to be with you and savor every flavor on your skin. I want a chance to
win you back and convince you of my love. Come to me, *querida*, give me more.

With everyone gone the halls were silent as I eased into your room and found you lounging
in the dark half undressed. Here, I said, I'll do the rest as I touched and teased your chest
and kissed you on the lips and neck and found your belt buckle cold against my breast as I
knelt to ease you from your too-snug jeans. I touched your tightness with my tongue until
you said, shall we shower first and wash the sweat and smell of show business away.

XXXVIII

Hot water rinsed the soap, prickled our skin, tickling our senses as we leaned into
the rushing fall and laughed beneath our hands, still trying to understand why we loved
the way we did, why we couldn't get enough of it, no matter how we tried. I never lied,
I said, when I told you that you mean the world to me and I don't know how I could be
alive and well and full of joy without you. It isn't you, you said. It isn't me. It's us.

There was something undeniably sweet about the way your feet danced me slowly into
the room and tipped me to the unmade bed, my head still wet, my nipples hard, my breath
laboring already from your kisses. We were down to counting hours and I wanted you so
badly I didn't want you to wait for me. But, you hushed me with more kisses, shushed
me with you fingers, until sated I lay shivering in my own sweat, waiting yet for you.

Luz, you are so beautiful, so perfect in your passion, so full of light, I'm charmed,
disarmed by who you are and what you mean to me. No, *querida*, don't move, don't
hurry me, I need to take my time because for once I'm going to linger inside you and
finger every cell until I know your taste so well I'll never forget how you feel around me.
Can you do that for me? Lie still. Just breathe and let me seek your heart, your soul.

XXXIX

This was a new role for me, one of passive receiver, and I didn't know how to play
the part. I stilled my legs and opened them wide. I stilled my arms and rested them
above my head. I stilled the beating of my heart and matched my breathing to the way
you sighed in and out, slick and hot. I stilled the thoughts pounding inside my head and
listened to the way you moved, sinuous, slow as a snake crawling on stone into the sun.

And there I was as you could see me with your inner eye, glowing pink and warm, every
muscle constricting to the pressure you slid into me, grasping then releasing, tickling
and teasing, until I felt I had to stir and meet you there. I twitched a toe and you said,
don't move. *Querida*, don't you dare move. Let me take you with me. Let me do the
work and feel you open all you are to me. Let me. *Querida*. Let me. Let me....

In the stillness, our breathing slow but ragged, you barely shifted your weight forward,
then pulled back, I felt you nudge me in a place where I'd never been touched before
and I soared upward to meet your spiral down and with gasp and groan we owned
the precious night, owned each other, owned our selves like no others had ever been
able to do. I felt you melt, merge into my skin, my blood, my bones and we were one.

XXXX

I wanted to cry, but I couldn't. I wanted to laugh, but I wouldn't disturb the afterglow
with sound of any kind. I just wanted to feel your heart pounding in my ear, feel you
so near I knew your thoughts and smiled. Still joined, you rolled us over and I moaned
at the pleasure of sheer motion, then rested there atop you, still pulsing, still enthralled.
I needed to see your face, you said, I needed to know that your delight's as great as mine.

It was an hour before we could bear to separate ourselves and stretch out beat upon
the bed. All our songs had been sung, the poetry all read. There was nothing left to talk
about, so we were silent as the night ticked on. But we couldn't stop touching each other's
skin as if to check and see if everything we'd done was really real. If I could steal one
moment, it would be the one where you touched my face, whispered beauty, then slept.

I curled closer to your side and thanked the gods for bringing you to me, for giving me this
great gift of seeing myself inside your eyes, of knowing I was truly loved and that nothing,
not time, or distance, or geography would ever keep us apart for long. I was your song.
You were my perfect poem. Together, matching my meter and rhyme with your lyrics and
melody, we'd find a way to go on wanting, go on giving, go on loving more and more.

Printed in the United States
44962LVS00007B/370-477

9 780977 127252